Front cover:
Yellow and Lilac Waterlilies
(detail). 1914–17, oil on
canvas, 200×215cm (cat 59)
The Toledo Museum of Art.
See page 52
Opposite:
The Garden
1900, oil on canvas,
81×92cm (cat 7)
Ralph T Coe
Overleaf: detail

Monet in the 20th Century: an introduction

Royal Academy of Arts

Sponsor's preface

The final year of the century is a good time to look back as well as forward, and Monet's paintings from the early years of this century will surely provide inspiration well into the next. They have found almost universal appeal and have become some of the best known and most widely reproduced images of our time.

We are delighted to work with the Royal Academy of Arts to help bring this superb exhibition of Monet in the 20th Century to its only European venue.

Nick Land
Chairman
ERNST & YOUNG

Christopher Yetton

Claude Monet
20th century painter

1

2

The catalogue numbers referred to in the essay and throughout the book are the numbers given to the works in the Royal Academy's exhibition. When a comparative figure in the essay also has a catalogue number, it is referred to by its figure number

A New Departure

In 1890–91, when he was 50, Monet painted a series of wheatstacks (fig 3) that was to prove a radical new departure in his work. It was the birth of his series method which he used for the remaining 36 years of his life. The two recent exhibitions covering the period of the series – Monet in the 90s, shown in 1990, and the current Monet in the 20th Century – have made it possible to grasp their power and complexity. It is only by seeing the works of each series hung together in exhibitions such as these that their qualities and meaning become apparent.

Each series was the result of a conscious decision to make a number of paintings from a single motif (or a set of closely related motifs) using a limited number of inter-related compositions. These compositions were simpler but more subtle and decorative than Monet's earlier work. At first he said that he was trying to capture 'the same light spreading everywhere', the 'ambience' and the 'atmosphere'. Although these sound like naturalistic concerns, they also point to an overall and abstract idea of pictorial harmony. He told a visitor to an exhibition of 15 of the wheatstacks in 1891 that a landscape did not exist in its own right since its aspect changed from moment to moment. Change itself became a greater concern for him than the specific details of the motif. He ceased to be interested in the scenic or the picturesque and instead became involved in a new degree of subjectivity and sought a deeper poetry in his work.

Paradoxically, as he developed the poetic and abstract qualities of his painting he also developed a deeper understanding of his response to nature. He insisted that the more he looked at the world, the stranger and more complex it appeared. This led him to reflect on his own nature. His explorations of painting and the natural world were also explorations of his own complexity, which he pursued with passion and detachment.

Gradually, from 1890 until his death in 1926 at the age of 86, Monet used colour with greater intensity to register simultaneously the light and his emotional response to nature, emphasising that he was trying 'to render what I feel'. He thought of each series as a whole and kept all of its paintings together, working on them as a group and keeping in mind the cumulative effect they would make when exhibited. The colour relationships were adjusted so that the paintings related to each other and maintained the unity of the series. This method had another paradoxical effect. Painting the works in relation to one another threw emphasis on the subtle ways they differ from each other. Thus attention is drawn to the individual qualities of the paintings. He emphasised the musical nature of the colour and the expressive qualities of the whole canvas rather than the subject matter. The poetic meaning of the subject emerged from the series rather than from individual paintings. He claimed 'instantaneity' as a goal but was prepared to spend several years working on a group of paintings in order to achieve it. His technique became increasingly complex and considered, with one colour dragged across another so that a painting could be made out of a number of interacting layers. But he also had a horror of formulated method and pushed his work forward by taking calculated risks.

With the exception of the *Grandes Décorations* in the Orangerie in Paris, the series were broken up when sold, so it is only in exhibitions like these that we can come to understand the work of his last 36 years, when he made almost 800 paintings out of his total output of 2,000. This substantial proportion of his oeuvre is 20th-century in its scope and ambition, and in the last 12 years of his life he increased both the size of his work and his brush strokes to produce some of the most radical paintings of the first quarter of the century, comparable with the developments of Matisse, Mondrian, Kandinsky or Picasso.

Importance of the Motif

Monet selected the small number of motifs he used between 1890 and 1926 very carefully. The more powerful and important the image, the slower the process of recognition, as we shall see with the water garden. He gradually understood an element of autobiography in his motifs. 'I am beginning to see myself a bit in what I do' he wrote to Rodin in 1889, and in the same year he told his wife that by looking at his painting of an old oak tree she would 'realise the rages and difficulties I have had (here)'.

Monet and Mallarmé: The Water Garden 1899–1900

In 1899 Monet produced 12 paintings of the Japanese bridge that spanned his water garden. Most are squarish in format with the bridge seen in profile and placed almost symmetrically on the canvas. This sense of symmetry, with the canvas divided in half by the far end of the pool, and the consequent stillness this evokes is carried over from the earlier Morning on the Seine series of 1896/97 (fig 4).

3

Fig 1
Rouen Cathedral, Sunlight Effect
1892–94
Museum of Fine Arts, Boston. Julia Cheney Edwards Collection

Fig 2
Poplars on the Banks of the River Epte
1891
Philadelphia Museum of Art. Bequest of Anne Thomson in memory of her father, Frank Thomson, and her mother, Mary Elizabeth Clarke Thomson

Fig 3
Wheatstack in the Sunlight
1891
Courtesy of Helly Nahmad Gallery, London

Fig 4
Arm of the Seine near Giverny in the Fog (Morning on the Seine)
1897
North Carolina Museum of Art, Raleigh. Purchased with funds from the Sarah Graham Kenan Foundation and the North Carolina Art Society (Robert F Phifer Bequest)

4

Fig 5
Water Lily Pond
1899
The National Gallery, London

Fig 6
The Water Lily Pond
1900 (cat 3)
Museum of Fine Arts, Boston. Given in memory of Governor Alvan T Fuller by the Fuller Foundation

In the construction of the bridge and water garden Monet was influenced by Japanese prints and garden design, but even more so by the poet Stéphane Mallarmé. Monet first met Mallarmé in 1886 and saw him often after that. They admired each other greatly and shared a lively correspondence. Mallarmé wrote to Monet in 1890 that he saw the fields through the memory of the wheatstacks which had so impressed him when he first saw them in Monet's studio. In the 1880s and 90s, Mallarmé was at the centre of artistic influence in Paris. Young writers like Marcel Proust, André Gide, Paul Claudel and Paul Valéry gathered round him, as did painters like Whistler and musicians like Debussy; Monet became part of this circle.

In 1885, Mallarmé had invited Monet, among other painters, to illustrate his prose poem 'The White Water Lily', and although he did not fulfil the commission it clearly made a profound impression on him. In the poem, Mallarmé described rowing along a little stream that, on entering a garden, broadens out into a still pool with water lilies, crossed by a single arched bridge. The pool had been designed by the garden's female owner and expressed her character. Monet's water garden, and its relationship to the little stream that feeds it, is so close to Mallarmé's poem that its construction in 1893 must have been influenced by it.

Mallarmé's death in 1898 may have brought the unfulfilled commission back to mind when Monet painted the first water garden series the following year. In the poem the rower's skiff runs aground on a clump of reeds at the entrance to the pool. The rower is just about to take another stroke, leaning forward looking at the straps which hold his feet, when he becomes aware that the sound of someone's footsteps has just ceased. He is held enthralled by the unseen presence of the owner as he is held by the straps holding his feet.

Monet's 1899 series calls this early part of the poem to mind. The paintings contain an abundance of plants: the trees surrounding the pond enclose it completely, the water lilies nearly fill the water surface, the bridge arches over it. Everything is still, brought to a halt by profusion and symmetry (fig 5). But the paintings have a greater autobiographical content than the poem. Monet was the creator of the water garden as well as its painter. The garden expresses his nature and the paintings can be seen as a kind of self portrait. In terms of the poem he would be the unseen owner as well as the rower of the skiff.

Monet returned to the subject of the Japanese bridge and pool in 1900 (fig 6) but in these later pictures he abandoned the symmetrical placing of the bridge. It seems he felt the 1899 paintings were too perfectly balanced and the new work implies a critique both of them and the Morning on the Seine series. In the 1900 paintings he intensified the feeling of profusion by lengthening the drags of paint and through the roughness of the application. He painted water irises across the front of

Fig 7
Charing Cross Bridge, Reflections on the Thames
1899–1904 (cat 13)
The Baltimore Museum of Art. The Helen and Abram Eisenberg Collection

some of them which have the effect of halting the eye. The colour is now dominated by a red/green combination rather than the blue/yellow of the earlier series. Red and green are traditionally associated with solid form, whereas blue/yellow are the colours of space. All these changes combine to arrest the spectator's eye. They are equivalent to the small island of reeds on which the skiff is stuck in Mallarmé's poem. They are the bar to entering the garden and encountering the mysterious owner, whose nature the garden expresses.

Memories of Horizons Part 1: London

Monet broke off from the water garden paintings to go to London to paint in autumn 1899, and from February to April in both 1900 and 1901, staying at the Savoy Hotel. There were several reasons why he chose London. He liked the city and the English, and associated both with freedom. He fled to London to escape the Franco-Prussian War in 1870, and his friend Emile Zola hid there in 1898 after being found guilty of libel in a trial arising from the Dreyfus affair.

London was not a ceremonial capital like Paris; it was the centre of an empire, the greatest industrial complex of the time and the largest and busiest port in the world. If Monet chose his motifs through a form of identification, then he must have identified with the freedom that London represented and the power it manifested.

Of the three motifs he chose, Waterloo Bridge most clearly shows London as a powerful industrial city (fig 8). The bridge itself is massive in its construction and forms a single powerful shape across the middle of the paintings. In the background the factory chimneys of Lambeth smoke, brewing the smog. The bridge is choked with traffic. London throbs.

In contrast, the Houses of Parliament are the emblem of Britain's political freedom. England's regard for individual liberty appealed to Monet, who hated the power of the state. All these elements interested him, but above all he loved London in the winter: 'In the summer it is fine, with the parks, but that does not compare with the winter.' The winter weather was necessary to reveal the deep bass notes of London's power.

A further factor in the choice of London was artistic rivalry. Monet was always conscious of the need to assert

Fig 8
Waterloo Bridge, Grey Weather
1903 (cat 18)
Copenhagen, Ordrupgaardsamlingen

himself, to take the artistic leadership in France. His development in the 1890s was in part to assert himself over the Neo-Impressionists and Gauguin and the Symbolists. In painting London he took on Whistler (another friend) and especially Turner. He later felt he came out on top.

Mist and Fog

Monet said that it was reflecting on a painting of a church in the mist that had first given him the idea of the series method. Mist both simplified the landscape, aiding the invention of the flatter and more decorative compositions that he sought, and also made the subtle and gradual changes in the light more visible. His use of mist in the 1890s is most clearly shown in the Morning on the Seine pictures. The mist in this series corresponds closely to a famous description of morning on the river by Corot, Monet's favourite 19th-century artist, which compares the pre-dawn landscape to a white-primed canvas (which Monet favoured after 1890): 'At the outset one does not see very much. Nature resembles a white-primed canvas on which the profile of a few massive shapes barely outline themselves: everything is hazy. One sees nothing… everything is there… the landscape is completely behind the transparent gauze of mist that lifts up and up and up, inhaled by the sun… finally one perceives everything that one guessed at first.' The mist in Corot's description obscures a deep space whose presence is sensed and eventually revealed. It introduced a sense of mystery.

In one of the Charing Cross bridge paintings (fig 7) we can see clear to a horizon that is obscured in the other London views. The knowledge of that deep space is an important part of this series.

But Monet's use of fog as a poetic image in the London series goes much deeper than this. It is again connected with Mallarmé. In his poem 'L'Azur', the fog is associated with both impotence and death. These are the first clues to the meaning of fog in Monet's London. Then there is Mallarmé's description of the journey to London in the first part of his lecture 'Music and Literature' (1894) which is titled 'A Worthwhile Journey'. 'The known journey ceased completely entering enveloping London. Its monumental fog cannot be separated from the idea of the city. No more than the light and the wind can lift it and roll it from the base of rough structures to just above the buildings only

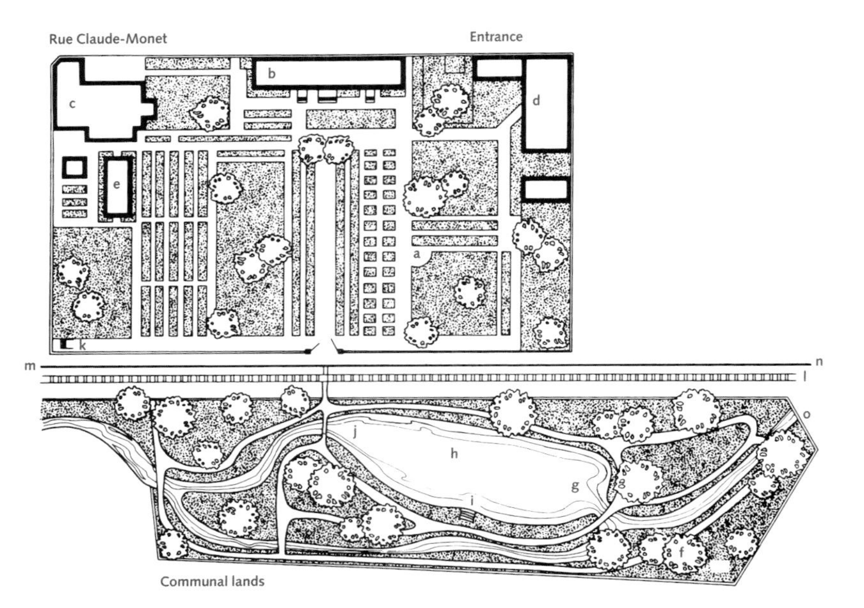

Map of Monet's property at Giverny after the 1902 alterations, but also showing the third studio (d) he had built in 1915

Plan of the Gardens

- a The 'Clos Normand'
- b The house
- c The second studio
- d The *Nymphéas* studio
- e The greenhouses
- f The water garden
- g Water duct for the pond
- h Water lily pond
- i Dock
- j Japanese footbridge
- k Underground passage connecting the gardens
- l Railroad
- m Road to Vernon
- n Road to Gasny
- o River Ru

to let it fall again, immense, superb and closed. The vapour seems liquid-like, to flow only a little way with the Thames.' Monet appears to echo these words when he told the dealer René Gimpel in 1918 that what he loved most about London was the fog: 'Without the fog, London would not be a beautiful city. It is fog that gives it its magnificent amplitude... it is a mass, an ensemble and it is so simple... its regular and massive blocks become grandiose in that mysterious mantle.' Common to both descriptions is the dual effect of the fog in monumentalising and making mysterious.

Mallarmé developed his image of fog in the magnificent 'Toast Funèbre' written on the death of Théophile Gautier, the poet who had trained as a painter and who wrote art criticism. Mallarmé wrote to a friend that he wanted to celebrate Gautier above all as one who saw – as a visionary, sighted man:

> 'Vast hollow carried in the mass of fog...
> Memories of horizons, O you, what is the Earth?
> Shouts this dream; and, like a voice whose clarity fades
> Space has for a toy the cry: "I do not know!"'

In the poem, to see clearly is to have the ability – both literally and metaphorically – to see to the horizon. The fog, by contrast, produces the sensation of a huge space that cannot be seen. There are only 'memories of horizons', of clear sight, and this raises the question, for someone like Gautier whose knowledge comes from seeing things, of what the world is. Mallarmé suggests that the fog, which he described earlier in the poem as a shroud on the dead poet, muffles the answer as to the nature of the world, and reduces it to a mere plaything.

Monet always insisted that his knowledge of the world came from his sight. He felt this so strongly that he had several episodes of hysterical blindness at times of great anxiety. His desire to paint London in the fog was a desire to paint when reduced by nature to near blindness which, for a painter like him, was a state of impotence. In an equivalent way to Mallarmé's dead poet, Monet, in his London series, had only the memory of a horizon which threw his understanding of the world into question and balanced his feelings of power and strength with a sensation of helplessness and a fear of death.

The sun is often attempting to break through in these paintings, although sometimes it is only dimly sensed. Most of them are painted against the light as though Monet was looking through the fog for the sun – the source of light, energy and hope. This means that most of the Waterloo Bridge series is painted in the morning looking eastwards from his Savoy Hotel balcony. The Charing Cross Bridge series is all painted in the afternoon looking west from the same balcony with the sun behind the bridge, and the Houses of Parliament in the late afternoon, painted from St Thomas's Hospital against the setting sun. The views in these directions and at these times of day are not accidental, and the search for the sun through the shrouding fog is a crucial element in their meaning.

The colour Monet used to register his emotions summoned up by winter in London is by turns subtle and dramatic. He started nearly 100 canvases and continued to work on them together when he returned to Giverny, until he exhibited 37 in May 1904. In 1903, he had written to his dealer Durand-Ruel from Giverny: 'I cannot send you a single canvas of London, because it is indispensable to have them all before me, and to tell the truth, not one is definitely finished. I develop them all together.' Monet had built up an astonishingly complex knowledge of light effects and how they could be achieved in paint. He developed a great range of colour from one painting to another. One painting would be dominated by blue and red, another by green and yellow. It was the overall effect of the series, when shown together, that he was concerned with. This is why it was important for Monet to see the paintings together and why it is still important to see

Fig 9
Water Lilies (The Clouds)
1903
Private Collection

Fig 10
Water Lilies
1904 (cat 26)
Denver Art Museum. Funds from the Helen Dill Bequest

9

10

them this way now. They feed off each other.

One more element of self-identification occurs in this series. In a number of them there are small boats, painted either singly or in pairs. They seem to embody Monet's feelings of isolation in the face of the extremely difficult and complex painterly task he had set himself, and when there are two boats – always a mirror image of each other – this only intensifies the feeling of loneliness and his position in front of the image of enshrouding death.

Memories of Horizons Part 2: The Water Lilies

When Monet returned from his last trip to London in 1901, he set about acquiring the land which enabled him to enlarge his water garden. He had first constructed the garden in 1893 but did not discover its true significance for his painting until some 10 years later. This lengthy gestation paid off in the realisation of the greatest of the series motifs which was to preoccupy him until his death. Perhaps it took him so long to realise its value as a motif because it also preoccupied him in his other celebrated role as a gardener.

In the new paintings after 1903, Monet altered the angle of his vision and, in a gesture that changed everything, instead of looking straight ahead to the horizon, turned his eyes down to the water surface. Thus his gaze became more like that of Narcissus. When Narcissus looked into the pool he did not only see himself. It is implicit in Ovid's myth that he would see the reflection of the trees surrounding his secluded glade, and presumably also the sky. When Monet looked at the pool's surface he saw his water lilies and the reflection of his garden, which already embodied himself in some degree. Alberti, in his treatise 'On Painting' (1435–36), described Narcissus as the first painter: 'The inventor of painting, according to the poets, was Narcissus, who was turned into a flower… what is painting but the act of embracing, by means of art, the surface of the pool?' In visual art the result of contemplating the reflection in the water is beauty – Narcissus is turned into a flower.

In Mallarmé's 'White Water Lily', the pool is referred to as 'this crystal'; it is the female owner's 'inner mirror' and its clarity is the 'limpidity of her glance'. Monet's 1904 paintings (fig 10) have this mirror-like quality to the water surface. Later in the poem, she is referred to as 'the Meditative, or the Proud, the Wild, the Gay (lady)'. By using capital letters for the adjectives turned into nouns, Mallarmé is elevating her into the divinity of place and her perpetual invisibility – present through absence in the reflections – is proper to a god and is a 'virgin absence'. Monet also stressed the meditative quality of the water garden and although he is himself the owner, there is also a sense of a divinity of place and the exploration of something unknown in this series.

Monet's gesture of lowering his glance is a poetic gesture full of meaning. The reflecting surface of water is, as Alberti suggested, emblematic of visual art as it distances things from us as a painting does. The lowering of the gaze also results, from 1905, in the horizon disappearing above the top of the paintings. Like the fog in the London series, this creates ambiguity and the clear, direct view of the world vanishes. The horizon becomes a memory in a new way – referred to by the horizontal floating lily pads.

Fig 11
Water Lilies
1905 (cat 28)
Museum of Fine Arts, Boston. Gift of Edward Jackson Holmes

Fig 12
Water Lilies
1907 (cat 34)
Private Collection, Japan

11

12

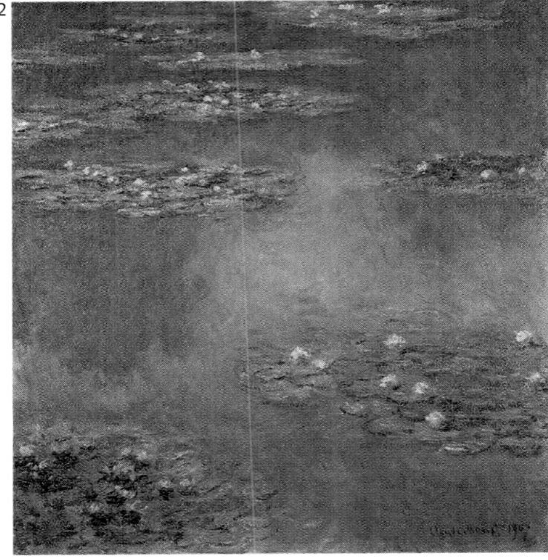

Reflections
In a 1904 painting (fig 10) Monet uses the plants on a sliver of bank at the top of the painting as a visual anchor – to stop the viewer getting lost in the mirror image. He also stressed the verticality of the reflected trees with upright strokes of paint. Verticality, with its reference to gravity, is an indication of reality and necessity. The painting thus has a quality of groundedness. The reflections are dominated by the surrounding trees. In later paintings he introduced an area of reflected sky. The problems involved in painting the sky in the realistic way he has treated the reflected trees is best illustrated by the 1903 painting (fig 9), which Monet is recorded as wanting to destroy. The sky is so illusionistically painted that we seem to fall into it. There is little to hold us; even the bank at the top of the picture cannot restrain the plunge. Monet overcomes this problem from 1905 onwards (fig 11) by painting the sky more flatly and more solidly.

The Sky as Subject
The gradual dominance of the reflected sky in the water lilies provides a new perspective on the earlier series. The fog turned the London pictures into sky paintings. The mists and reflections do the same for the Morning on the Seine series. The poplars (fig 2) with their horizontal slivers of land and slender vertical tree trunks are all sky. Even the solid wheatstacks (fig 3) float in 'the ambience', the 'atmosphere'. Geffroy's introduction to the catalogue for the 1891 exhibition refers to the stacks as 'transitory objects' on which are marked, as on the surface of a mirror, 'environmental influences, atmospheric effects, wandering breezes and short-lived light effects'. This all shows that the emergence of the sky as subject is a long process of gradual recognition culminating in the development of the water lily pool motif.

The Decorative
There is a gradual increase in the decorative quality of the first Water Lily series (1903–08, figs 10–14). This had been an important issue for Monet since 1890 and for French painting generally in this period. The issue of the decorative centred on the suppression of natural detail and the illusion of space in order to express something more profound and thought out. Monet tackled this from 1890 onwards by emphasising the composition, both in terms of colour relationships and the relative flatness of design – the exaltation of colour as an emotional experience and the choice of subjects that embodied a contemplative form. The series method itself threw the emphasis on to the abstract qualities of the repeated composition.

The Poplar series is perhaps the most obviously decorative of the 1890s works (fig 2). The tops of the trees form an 'S' shape as they follow the serpentine river into the distance. This is played off against the verticals of the foreground trunks. The decorative effect is so striking that a contemporary observer referred to them as the 'whirl' series. In front of these works it is easy to remember that

Fig 13
Water Lilies
1907 (cat 39)
The Museum of Fine Arts, Houston. Gift of Mrs Harry C Hanszen

Fig 14
Water Lilies
1908 (cat 46)
Maspro Denkoh Art Museum

Monet's favourite painter was Watteau, and there is something rococo in the flourish of the poplars.

In the first Water Lily series (1903–08), Monet played a series of variations. There are groups based on particular patterns of water lilies or shapes of reflected sky. There are also variations in the format of the pictures. In a group of nearly square paintings he sometimes makes the horizontal measurement greater than the vertical (fig 11), and sometimes the vertical greater than the horizontal (fig 12). There is a wonderful cycle of paintings in 1907 where he used the vertical format to increase the sense of downward movement following a river of light, but slowed it with a group of lily pads painted right across the middle of the reflected sky (fig 13). These pads also hold our eyes on the surface of the painting. In 1908, he made a masterly series of variations of horizontal and vertical squares coupled with amazing flatness and colour (fig 14, cat 47).

At the same time the artist experimented with a circular format. This removed the viewer's reference to gravity and the horizon provided by the vertical and horizontal sides of the conventional rectangular format. However, we can see why Monet abandoned this experiment. The horizontals of the water lily pads were unable to hold the composition, and they appear to slip around in the pictures (cat 38). This format over-emphasised the floating and drifting qualities that worked so well in the other more conventionally shaped canvases.

Colour

The increase in flatness that is apparent in the paintings from 1905 onwards is accompanied by an increase in colour. The areas of reflected sky provided an opportunity for this. It began delicately in 1905 (fig 11) with the 1890s idea of the 'same light spreading everywhere' being slowly replaced by the feeling of colour spreading everywhere (fig 12). For some time the two ideas were interchangeable but gradually the sensation of colour becomes overwhelming (fig 14). The vertical paintings of 1907 were crucial in this respect. Colour treated as an area was intensified in the reflected sky (cat 42) and spread from there like a blush throughout the whole painting (cat 43). The contrast of colours became emphasised as between the reds of the water lilies and the green of the pads (fig 13). This was developed further in 1908 (fig 14) when the contrast of tone was abandoned, to be replaced by colour of a similar tone and intensity which was spread across the surface of the paintings.

Painting and Music

Critical writing in the 1890s and early 20th century emphasised the correspondence between the arts. Firmin Javal wrote in 1892 about the poplars: 'Never… has the great landscapist revealed himself more a great poet, a great musician, that is to say a great painter, than in these 15 pages.' Monet also thought in those terms. The 1890s series are each equivalent to a song cycle or group of poems. The London series is in three movements:

Fig 15
The Water Lily Pond
1915–26, oil on canvas,
diptych: 200×300cm each
(cat 88)
Kunsthaus Zürich.
Right: detail

15

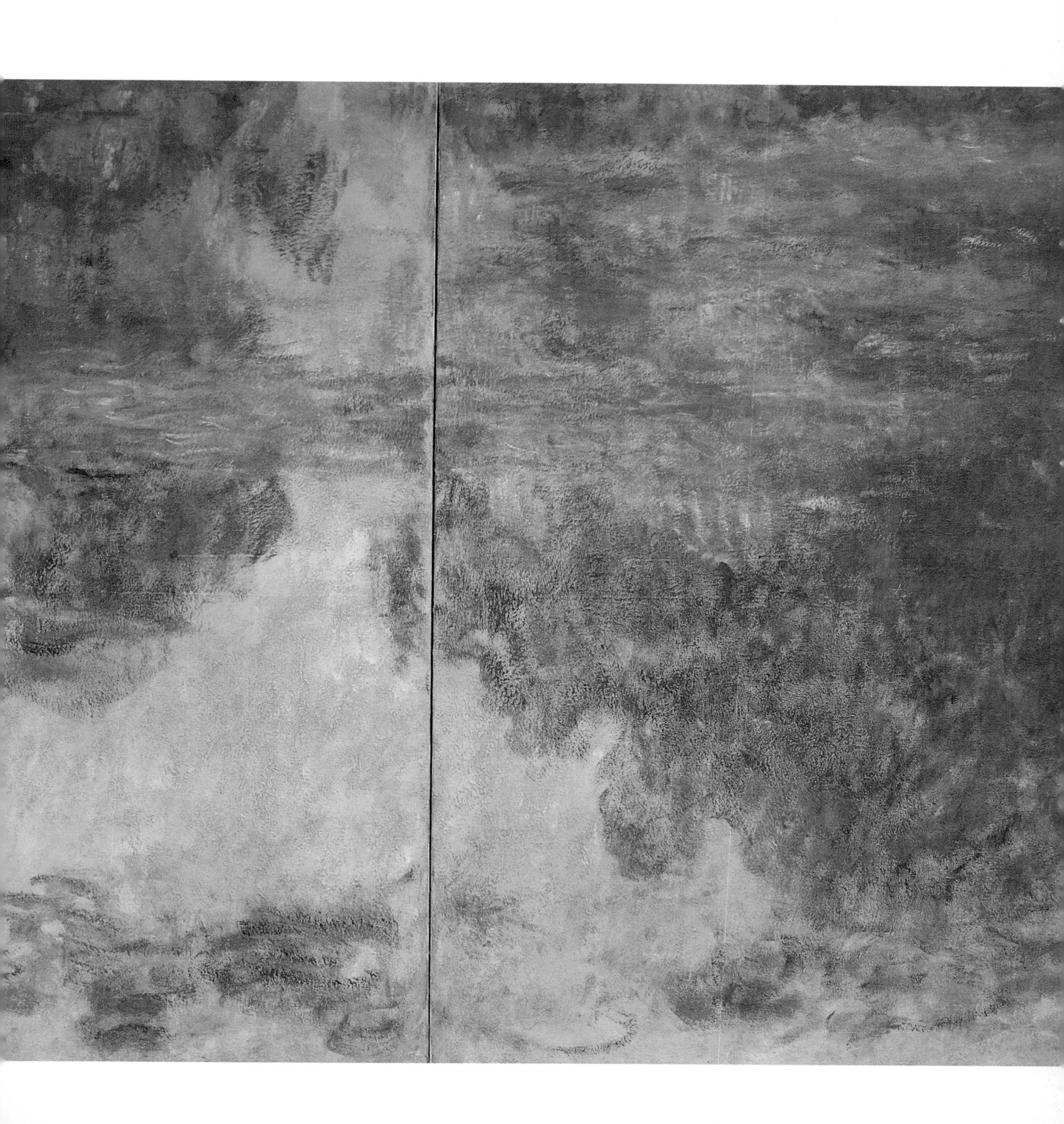

Fig 16
Wassily Kandinsky, Composition No 7
1913
Tretyakov Gallery, Moscow

Waterloo Bridge, Charing Cross Bridge and the Houses of Parliament. Expressed in another way, these could be seen as morning, afternoon and evening. The first Water Lily series (1903–08) is a vast song cycle with many smaller groupings within it, for example the vertical format paintings of 1907 (fig 13, cat 42, 43) or a group from 1908 (fig 14, cat 47). In 1891, the young Valéry wrote to Mallarmé to express his admiration for 'L'Après-Midi d'un Faune': 'The supreme idea is now gaining ground of a lofty symphony uniting the world around us with the inner world that haunts us.' From the 1890s Monet wanted to unite these two worlds, increasing his concern with the inner world while maintaining his allegiance to the outer. He found his poetic imagery in nature and relied on vision to guide him. In this way he is comparable to Matisse and Bonnard. He is never willing to relinquish the idea of the visual exploration of the world. This distinguished him from Symbolists like Emile Bernard or Paul Gauguin and is the reason that he always insisted, however untruthfully, that he worked in front of nature.

Mallarmé, and the artists who gathered round him – Claudel, Proust, Gide, Mirbeau, Débussy and Whistler – all used musical terms to discuss the highest forms of art, and saw Wagner as music's greatest exemplar. It is following this lead that Kandinsky, when he first saw a wheatstack in Moscow in 1896, described in his 1913 'Reminiscences' the revelatory spiritual power coming from its colour and wildness by pairing it with his first hearing of 'Lohengrin' and his desire to paint Moscow as a 'symphony'. In 'Concerning the Spiritual in Art' of 1912, he called for a new 'symphonic composition' and proposed that such a composition be 'subjected to a principal form' that derived its 'inner resonance' by being, as the wheatstacks had been for him, 'hard to detect'. He also listed three different sources of inspiration for this symphonic composition which surely derive from his reaction to Monet: '1. a direct impression of nature, 2. a spontaneous and unconscious improvisation' (his view of Monet's techniques), 'and 3. a slowly worked expression of inner feeling' (Monet's ambition for his series).

In the 1950s, Clement Greenberg redirected art criticism when he picked up Valéry's and Kandinsky's term 'symphonic' to advocate the loose, open, painterly structure he saw in both late Monet and the new Abstract Expressionism. Monet's influence on 20th-century art was pervasive. After him most 20th-century painters in general felt that painting as an activity, by its very nature, happened in series.

Venice: A Tourist Interlude

In 1908, Monet went with his wife to Venice. At the time he was very depressed about the Water Lily series and reluctantly agreed to the trip, saying it was only to please her. He stayed just over two months, eventually overcoming his initial reluctance to produce some 40 paintings. It is likely that he had often thought about painting Venice. It was an ideal subject for him: a city famous for its light, suspended between water and sky with a long history of being painted by some of the great painters of Western art who Monet felt he could measure himself against. But although he found some interesting colour combinations the series never attained the intensity of the London paintings. No powerful poetic images or elements surfaced through which he could focus his deeper concerns. Part of the trouble was expressed in the preface to the exhibition catalogue in 1912 by Octave Mirbeau. Venice was no longer a true city – it was tourist décor. It was very difficult to see Venice with fresh eyes. Perhaps the problem was that there was no contemporary inspiration. Venice's greatness was in the past. But at least going to Venice allowed him to see his water lilies afresh, and after he returned he was able to put together the exhibition of water lilies, calling the series Water Landscapes, in 1909.

Monet did eventually finish 29 of the Venice paintings in the winter of 1911–12 for an exhibition the following May, but he was not happy with the results. 'I know beforehand that you'll say my pictures are perfect. I know that when they are shown they will be much admired but I don't care because I know they are bad,' he wrote to

Durand-Ruel in 1912.The failure of the Venice series to achieve the poetic power of the London paintings or the water lilies illustrates how important it was for Monet not only to have the right motif but also to have a way of approaching it to engage his deepest response. He needed something like the London fog or the mirroring of water to both involve and distance him.

A New Kind of Painting

Monet produced very little painting in the five years between the exhibition of the water lilies in May 1909 and the summer of 1914. This was a time of personal tragedy. He was devastated by the death of his wife, Alice, in May 1912 from spinal leukaemia, and by his son Jean's stroke in the same year.

But by June 1914, the passion to paint had returned, and he was hard at work on a project for a decorative panorama of water lilies that he had had in mind on and off since first mentioning it in an interview with Maurice Guillemot in 1897: 'Imagine a circular room in which the dado is completely covered by an expanse of water dotted with aquatic flora.' At the time Monet was working on the Morning on the Seine series, whose flat decorative nature may well have prompted the ambition to paint true decorations. Roger Marx, in an interview with Monet in 1909 (based on earlier conversations), quoted Monet as saying, 'One moment the temptation came to me – use the water lilies theme for the decoration of a room: carried the length of the walls, completely covering the wall panels in its unity.' Monet's comment later in this interview that 'nerves overstrained by work would have been soothed there, in harmony with the restful example of these still waters' recalls Matisse's 1908 'Notes of a Painter', and his famous desire for an art of balance 'devoid of troubling subject matter' that would provide rest for the mind 'like a good armchair'. Monet never lost touch with the latest developments in art.

The outbreak of the First World War in August, shortly after he had resumed working, appalled him but he felt, like Matisse, who visited him during the War, that his duty was to paint.

The five fallow years of 1909–14 had prepared the most dramatic development of Monet's career. In 1914, he began a number of studies that were generally twice the size of his earlier water lilies. They were painted very broadly, with large brushes. The increase in size accompanied by the larger brush strokes led to a very different kind of painting. The individual mark now registered as an area of colour. The flatness of these marks was related to an overall sense of flatness – appropriate for wall decorations – and the space depicted became much more closely related to the surface of the canvases. In the first studies (cat 60) he explored vertical and horizontal relationships across this new large surface. He also investigated the effects of large areas of flat-ish colours with strong colour contrasts so that the paintings became constructed with colour to a far greater degree than before (cat 63). In these works a consideration of drawing that had been present but not stressed in his earlier water lilies now came to the fore. In the terms Matisse used much later, the problem was to find the 'painterly sign' for things. What was the simplified sign for a lily pad, a water lily flower, the reflection of a weeping willow? These simplified signs would be a necessary part of a large decoration. This group of paintings was a reconsideration of the water lily compositions of 1903–08 but on a far larger scale.

In the most exciting of the studies of 1916–19, he looked at the reflection of the trunk of a young weeping willow outlined by light (cat 66). In these, the long strokes of paint act simultaneously as both colour and drawing. They create a sense of light by their contrasts, a fullness of colour through their physical extent and form through their drawing. In this way Monet brought colour and drawing together as one. Traditionally drawing had been in monochrome and described form, while colour was seen as a separate and decorative element. Certain painters were celebrated for their drawing, others for their colour. Therefore it became an ideal to bring them together and make them one, an ideal pursued by, among others, Cézanne and Matisse. Monet's new method also created a new musicality from the contrast of colour, and the size gave grandeur to this music. Although these paintings are studies, many of them were worked on over a period of time. They are very considered, full of exciting painterly ideas. They also embody a clear expression of Monet's thoughts about painting at this time, and his ability to push painting forward.

Eye Problems

In 1912 Monet had suddenly felt he could not see out of his right eye. A cataract was diagnosed. However, this does not seem to have been as serious as he first thought. He

Fig 17
The Path under the Rose Arches
1918–24 (cat 85)
Private Collection, Switzerland

Fig 18
The Artist's House seen from the Rose Garden
1922–24 (cat 86)
Musée Marmottan – Claude Monet, Paris

17

18

had had difficulty with his sight before. In 1867, a fortnight before the birth of his son, Jean, when he was separated from his mistress, Camille, he became temporarily blind and was afraid he would be unable to paint outside again. In 1908, his sight had become blurred and he experienced vertigo which his wife, Alice, thought was due to anxiety about the Water Lily series. In early January 1910, he told Geffroy that he saw 'everything black'. From 1913–19 he did not mention eye problems except to say that his sight was good. He again complained about his vision in 1919 but was also working happily at times between 1920–22. In fact, it is impossible to disentangle the truth about Monet's sight from his emotional state both about his painting and his personal life. He eventually had two operations in January 1923 to remove the cataract in the right eye, after which he experienced colour distortion as the surgeon told him he would. He was a very impatient convalescent and was in despair that the operation had not cured him immediately. He had a third operation in July, and with time and new glasses his sight returned, allowing him to paint until his final illness in 1926.

Contrary to the opinion of many observers, his late paintings do not exhibit faults due to eye defects. The colour relationships are not distorted but embody his intentions, as the current exhibition shows, and he continued to develop his painting right to the end of his life. Monet had a very volatile temperament – he was always likely to feel he might never paint again. Considering the importance to him of his sight, it was not surprising that he was so anxious about the state of his eyes and, as his eye surgeon knew, his statements about them could not always be taken at face value.

Easel Paintings 1917–1926

Monet continued to make other series paintings at the same time as he was painting the wall decorations which incorporated, on a smaller scale, the changes he made to his working method. The most important were probably begun in 1917–18.

He produced a series of Water Lily paintings (cat 71) that have large areas of colour and the new freer drawing, linking the surface across the paintings in a loose series of interlocking gestures. There is also the series of Weeping Willows of 1918–19 which is amongst the most exciting painting done in France, or anywhere else, at the end of the First World War when there was a tendency amongst many artists to be less wild or experimental. Monet became even more daring. In old age the world appeared stranger and more mysterious to him than when he was younger.

In the 10 (largely) finished works (cat 82, 83) we see the tree quite close up from inside the tent of its foliage. The canopy forms a barrier across most of the painting. It is as though Monet was peering through the foliage looking for the light in the same way that he had looked for the sun through the fog in the London series. The dark, cave-like shape of the tree was a new poetic image for blindness, as the fog had been in the earlier series. Monet once said that he wished he had been born blind and regained his sight just before painting. The onset of his cataracts would have given a new sharpness to this idea. The only clear space is

Fig 19
The Japanese Bridge
1919–24 (cat 80)
The Minneapolis Institute of Arts. Bequest of Putnam Dana McMillan

19

at the bottom of these pictures. We seem to have to stoop down to see out, on the right of the canvas, across the corner of the lily pond. The paintings are astonishingly fierce, strong and optimistic. Monet, at the age of 80, seemed to identify with the tree – the strength of the trunk supporting the fall of the matted grief of the foliage. The looping vertical strokes are a marvellous way of combining colour and drawing on the scale of a large easel painting. They also link the painting across its surface, even being used in the solid trunk of the tree.

The late Japanese Bridge series (fig 19) was begun at about the same time as the weeping willows but was possibly continued longer, until 1924 or 1925. There are 24 of them, many finished, although some are clearly not. They are generally smaller than the weeping willows and their powerful painterly energy is very tightly held. Monet painted warm ones and cool ones. As in the weeping willows we see into the distance at the bottom of the paintings. The top is impenetrable – a mass of energy. We see into the distance only under the bridge. This is a new poetic image for the attempt to see the horizon, to explore the world and know it. It is interesting and mysterious that the way forward for Monet was across water.

These paintings are the most poetically powerful of the late easel series. The two themes – a tree and a bridge – are amongst the most common of his motifs throughout his life. It seems that both were powerful images for him, one of growth and life – enduring for many years – the other, a means to pass over an impassable obstacle, invariably water, a connecting link between two separated areas as between reality and the dream. In these late bridges, as in the London series, we concentrate on the bridge, not the land it connects.

There are also a number of late paintings of the garden near the house. The Path under the Rose Arches series (fig 17) also involves peering into an impenetrable mass

20

Fig 20
Green Reflections
1916–26
Musée de l'Orangerie des Tuileries, Paris.
One of the sections which make up the *Grandes Décorations*

with the space, along the path, in the lower part of the pictures. The Artist's House seen from the Rose Garden series (fig 18) has warm and cool varieties, and constitutes a new and more powerful use of colour than any earlier works. They reveal yet another new development in his painting and have a fresh exuberance and energy.

The Grandes Décorations

In the various series exhibitions Monet had explored the idea of a single work made out of multiple works. There had always been a strong sense of loss when these had been sold individually, making the intended experience impossible to recapture, except in exhibitions like the present one. The Orangerie decorations were Monet's solution to this problem. They introduced a new idea into the notion of the exhibition of art. They were a new way of framing his ideas and were unlike any other decorative ensemble of paintings.

At some point around 1914–16 Monet decided to make the wall decorations two metres high. He built a new studio big enough to both paint them in and see them together in the arrangement he wanted. In 1918, he decided to give them to France as an homage to his friend Georges Clemenceau, the French leader, and as a celebration of the end of the war. There was more than one site proposed for the scheme, but finally the decorations were installed in two elliptical rooms in the Orangerie of the Tuileries gardens. He painted far more panels than any of the schemes required – about 40 in all – of which 22 were finally used. The unused panels are in various states of finish.

Monet had enormous ambitions for this project and he was determined to realise them, working and reworking the paintings to achieve his aims. He must have had terrible fears that his eye troubles or ill health would intervene to frustrate his plans. He resisted all attempts to persuade him to stop reworking, which his friends feared would result in him ruining what he had already achieved. His courage, however, was greater than theirs. Although there may be some small difficulties in the fitting together of some of the canvases in the Orangerie, the work was basically finished before his death.

An unfinished diptych (fig 15) gives an idea of how his thoughts were developing. The sheer size of a painting

Overleaf:
Henri Manuel, photograph of Monet in his third studio in front of *Morning*, 1924–25, Archives Durand-Ruel, Paris

like this allowed Monet to deploy huge areas of colour. It also enabled him to create an enormous water surface. The size itself provided him with a new and fascinating problem: how to link together such a vast painting, and how to achieve unity across such a great horizontal expanse. Fig 15 shows part of the solution. He made broad areas of colour into large interlocking shapes with strong suggestions of flatness. On layers separate from this he used his new colour drawing to link across the underlying areas of colour. This can be seen in a more developed form in one of the 4.25 metre panels (cat 91), which has a complexity and ambiguity that is perhaps greater than anything in the Orangerie. The hanging fronds of the weeping willow on the right-hand side interact so subtly with the reflection of other trees that it is almost impossible to disentangle them. But the drawing across the surface links the painting in a marvellously loose and free way. The vast planes of space and colour are comparable with Wagner's vast plains of sound. The decorations are symphonic. They are a fulfilment of Valéry's call to Mallarmé in 1891 for the 'lofty symphony uniting the world around us with the inner world that haunts us'.

A further linking across the enormous surfaces of the Orangerie is by the floating groups of lily pads. But as Monet said, using a musical term, 'they are just the accompaniment. The essence of the motif is the mirror of water whose appearance alters at every moment.' The world of gravity and necessity is present in the reflections of the trees and other plants surrounding the pool, but Monet emphasised the 'patches of sky which are reflected'. In the Orangerie the reflections of the sky dominate. By pursuing his perception of the world, Monet has come to an expression of vastness. As he said to Georges Clemenceau, 'Your error is to wish to reduce the world to your measure, whereas by enlarging your knowledge of things you will find your knowledge of self enlarged.' By concentrating on reflections of the sky on this scale he introduced a sense of measure which is outside the ordinary human scale.

At the end of his life Monet, like Mallarmé, was haunted by the sky, and in his final extraordinary achievement he painted a vision of the world that revealed man's nature, like the sky, to be immense.

The Bridge over the Water Lily Pond
1900, oil on canvas,
89×100cm (cat 1)
The Art Institute of Chicago,
Mr and Mrs Lewis Coburn
Memorial Collection.
Right: detail

The Water Lily Pond (Symphony in Rose)
1900, oil on canvas, 90×100cm (cat 2)
Musée d'Orsay, Paris.
Legacy of Comte Isaac da Camondo, 1911.
Right: detail

Charing Cross Bridge, Overcast Weather
1900, oil on canvas, 60×92cm (cat 9)
Museum of Fine Arts, Boston. Given by Janet Hubbard Stevens in memory of her mother, Janet Watson Hubbard

Charing Cross Bridge, The Thames
1903, oil on canvas,
73×100cm (cat 10)
Musée des Beaux-Arts, Lyon

Waterloo Bridge, Sunlight Effect
1903, oil on canvas,
73×92cm (cat 20)
Milwaukee Art Museum,
Gift of Mrs Albert T. Friedmann.
Right: detail

Houses of Parliament, Sunset
1902, oil on canvas,
81×92cm (cat 20a)
Private Collection

Houses of Parliament, Sunset
1904, oil on canvas,
81×92cm (cat 24)
Kunsthaus Zürich.
Donation Walter Haefner

Water Lilies
1903, oil on canvas,
81×100cm (cat 25)
The Dayton Art Institute.
Gift of Mr Joseph Rubin.
Right: detail

Water Lilies
1905, oil on canvas,
73×105cm (cat 30)
Private Collection

Water Lilies
1908, oil on canvas,
diameter 81cm (cat 38)
Dallas Museum of Art.
Gift of the Meadows
Foundation, Incorporated

Water Lilies
1907, oil on canvas,
105×73cm (cat 42)
Göteborg Museum of Art,
Göteborg, Sweden

Water Lilies
1907, oil on canvas,
100×73cm (cat 43)
Bridgestone Museum of Art,
Ishibashi Foundation, Tokyo.
Following page: detail

Water Lilies
1908, oil on canvas,
100×81cm (cat 47)
National Museum and
Gallery, Cardiff

Water Lilies
1908, oil on canvas,
92×81cm (cat 48)
Mr G. Callimanopulos

The Grand Canal
1908, oil on canvas,
73×92cm (cat 51)
Museum of Fine Arts,
Boston. Bequest of
Alexander Cochrane

The Palazzo Contarini
1908, oil on canvas,
92×81cm (cat 58)
Kunstmuseum, St. Gallen,
Switzerland

Yellow and Lilac Water Lilies
1914–17, oil on canvas,
200×215cm (cat 59)
The Toledo Museum of Art.
Purchased with funds from
the Libbey Endowment,
Gift of Edward Drummond
Libbey

Water Lilies
1914–17, oil on canvas,
200×200cm (cat 60)
Private Collection

Water Lilies
1914–17, oil on canvas,
180×200cm (cat 63)
Asahi Breweries, Ltd

The Path in the Iris Garden
1914–17, oil on canvas,
200×150cm (cat 69)
The National Gallery,
London

Water Lilies, Reflections of Weeping Willows
1916–19, oil on canvas, 100×200cm (cat 66)
Benesse Corporation, Okayama, Japan

Claude Monet

The Water Lily Pond
1918–22, oil on canvas,
100×200cm (cat 71)
Musée des Beaux-Arts de
Nantes, Nantes, France

Claude Monet 1917

The Water Lily Pond
begun 1918, oil on canvas,
100×200cm (cat 72)
Honolulu Academy of Arts.
Purchased in memory of
Robert Allerton, 1966

The Japanese Bridge
1919–24, oil on canvas,
89×116cm (cat 78)
European Private Collection

Weeping Willow
1918–19, oil on canvas,
100×120cm (cat 83)
Kimbell Art Museum,
Fort Worth, Texas

Weeping Willow
1918, oil on canvas,
130×110cm (cat 82)
Columbus Museum of Art,
Ohio. Gift of Howard D.
and Babette L. Sirak, the
Donors to the Campaign
for Enduring Excellence,
and the Derby Fund.
Right: detail

Water Lily Pond
1916–26, oil on canvas,
200×425cm (cat 91)
The National Gallery,
London

	1840s	1850s	1860s	1870s
The life and art of Claude Monet	**1840** Oscar Claude Monet born on 14 November at 45 rue Laffitte, Paris. **1845** The family moves to Ingouville outside Le Havre, Normandy. Monet's father joins the business run by his brother-in-law, Jacques Lecadre, a wholesale merchant and ship's chandler.	**1856** Monet exhibits some of his caricatures at an artists' material shop. The proprietor introduces him to Eugène Boudin, who has a lasting influence on his professional career. **1857** Monet's mother dies. Monet and his elder brother, Léon, are now looked after by their aunt, an amateur painter.	**1860** Attends the Académie Suisse in Paris and meets Camille Pissarro. **1861** Drafted into military service, joins a cavalry regiment and is sent to Algeria where he contracts typhoid; is bought out of the army by his aunt. Convalescing in Le Havre, works with Boudin and Jongkind. Together they practise *plein-air* painting. Returns to Paris and enrols in the studio of Charles Gleyre, where he meets Pierre-Auguste Renoir, Alfred Sisley and Frédéric Bazille. **1864** Leaves Gleyre's studio which ends his formal education. **1865** Two paintings accepted for the first time at the Paris Salon. **1866** Shows again at the Salon. **1867** Penniless, he goes to stay with his family. His mistress, Camille, who is pregnant, remains in Paris, where their son Jean is born on 8 August. **1868** His work is again accepted at the Salon.	**1870** Rejected by the Salon. In June he marries Camille. They flee from the war to London. **1871** Meets up with Pissarro. Two paintings rejected by the RA's Summer Exhibition. His father dies. Returns to France via Zaandam in Holland, and settles in Argenteuil on the Seine to the west of Paris. **1874** The first Impressionist exhibition meets with a mixed reception. Monet's *Impression, Sunrise* is widely discussed and the artists become known as the 'Impressionists'. **1876** He shows in the second Impressionist exhibition. Invited by Ernest and Alice Hoschedé to their château at Montgeron. **1877** Exhibits 30 paintings in the third group show in April. **1878** Birth of his second son, Michel, on 17 March. Sets up joint household in Vétheuil with the Hoschedés after Ernest's bankruptcy the previous year. **1879** Monet contributes 29 paintings to the fourth group show in April. Camille dies on 5 September.
A context of events	**1840** Birth of Emile Zola and Auguste Rodin. **1842** Honoré de Balzac begins *La Comédie humaine* series of novels. **1847** Britain: Charlotte Brontë, *Jane Eyre*. **1848** Revolution throughout Europe. In France this leads to abdication of the King, Louis-Philippe. Second Republic established. Louis-Napoleon elected president. Germany: Karl Marx and Friedrich Engels, *The Communist Manifesto*. Britain: The Pre-Raphaelite Brotherhood is formed.	**1851** *Coup d'état* of Louis-Napoleon. Great Exhibition at the Crystal Palace, London. Death of JMW Turner. **1852** Napoleon III proclaims the Second Empire. Baron Haussmann begins the redevelopment of Paris. **1854** Crimean War begins (to 1856). **1855** Universal Exposition in Paris. Gustave Courbet organises his own exhibition and publishes his *Realist Manifesto*. **1857** Charles Baudelaire, *Les Fleurs du mal*; Gustave Flaubert, *Madame Bovary*. **1859** War between France and Austria. Britain: Charles Darwin, *On the Origin of Species*; Charles Dickens, *A Tale of Two Cities*.	**1861** Italy: Victor Emmanuel becomes King of united Italy. USA: Start of Civil War (to 1865). **1862** Victor Hugo, *Les Misérables*. Britain: International Exhibition is held in London. **1863** Salon des Refusés includes Edouard Manet's *Déjeuner sur l'Herbe*. Death of Eugène Delacroix. Charles Baudelaire, *The Painter of Modern Life*. **1865** Britain: Lewis Carroll, *Alice's Adventures in Wonderland*. **1866** Prussian defeat of Austria results in a major shift in the European balance of power. Russia: Dostoevsky, *Crime and Punishment*. **1867** Universal Exposition in Paris. Courbet and Manet display their work in independent pavilions. Death of Baudelaire. Mexico: Execution of Maximilian, Napoleon III's puppet emperor. Sweden: Alfred Nobel invents dynamite. **1869** Suez Canal opens. Birth of Henri Matisse. Russia: Tolstoy publishes *War and Peace* in book form.	**1870** France declares war on Prussia. French defeat at Sedan. Paris besieged by the Prussian army. Bazille killed in the war. USA: Foundation of the Metropolitan Museum of Modern Art in New York. **1871** Paris capitulates. Parisians declare an independent, socialist Commune on 18 March, which is bloodily suppressed in May by the government, based in Versailles. Franco-Prussian peace treaty agreed in May in which France cedes Alsace and Lorraine. Britain: George Eliot, *Middlemarch*. **1873** The Prussian army of occupation leaves French territory. Napoleon III dies in England. **1876** Stéphane Mallarmé, *L'Après-midi d'un faune*. Germany: First complete performance of Richard Wagner's *Ring of the Nibelung* at Bayreuth. USA: Alexander Graham Bell invents the telephone. **1877** Death of Courbet. USA: Thomas Edison invents phonograph. **1878** Death of Daubigny. **1879** Norway: Ibsen, *A Doll's House*.

1880s

1880 Does not participate in fifth group show but exhibits a painting at the Salon for first time in 10 years, causing a rift with some Impressionist friends.
1881 Does not show in sixth group exhibition. In December moves with Alice and the eight children, including his two sons, to Poissy.
1882 Has 35 pictures in the seventh group show.
1883 Rents a house in Giverny. Visits Cézanne at l'Estaque.
1884 Painting trip to the Mediterranean coast.
1886 Visits Holland in April. Does not participate in eighth group show in May. Travels to Belle-Ile off the coast of Brittany in the autumn.
1888 Travels to Antibes in the spring; also visits London.
1889 Paints in the Creuse valley in the Massif Central in the spring.

1880 First Boer War.
1881 Freedom of the press established in France.
Control of the Salon passes from the state to the Society of French Artists.
Spain: Birth of Pablo Picasso.
USA: Henry James, *The Portrait of a Lady*.
1883 Death of Manet.
Germany: Nietzsche, *Also Sprach Zarathustra*.
Britain: Machine gun patented by American-born Hiram S Maxim.
1886 Zola publishes *L'Oeuvre*, upsetting many of his artist friends who see themselves in its unattractive and unsuccessful hero, Claude Lantier.
1888 USA: George Eastman introduces the Kodak camera.
1889 Centennial of the French Revolution is marked by a Universal Exposition in Paris. The Eiffel Tower is its lasting symbol. General Boulanger, a right-wing politican, fails in his attempt to seize power and flees to Brussels.

1890s

1890 Starts campaign to buy Manet's *Olympia* for the state. Buys house and garden at Giverny for 22,000 francs.
1891 The first of his 'series', the *Wheatstacks*, is shown to great acclaim. Starts *Poplars* series. Death of Ernest Hoschedé.
1892 Begins *Rouen Cathedral* series. Marries Alice Hoschedé.
1894 Paul Cézanne and Mary Cassatt visit Giverny.
1895 Goes to Norway visiting his stepson Jacques Hoschedé. Paints Mount Kolsaas.
1896 Paints at Pourville on the Normandy coast and starts the *Morning on the Seine* series.
1897 At Pourville again, January – April. Jean Monet marries Blanche Hoschedé.
1898 *Morning on the Seine* shown at Georges Petit's gallery. Visits London to see his son, Michel, who is ill.
1899 Starts the *Japanese Bridge* series. To London in September to paint views of the Thames from the Savoy Hotel. Death of Suzanne Hoschedé-Butler.

1890 Death of Vincent van Gogh.
1891 Death of Georges Seurat. Paul Gauguin arrives in Tahiti.
1892 Emile Zola, *La Debâcle*, his study of the 1871 Franco-Prussian War.
Russia: Tchaikovsky, *The Nutcracker*.
1893 Norway: Edvard Munch paints *The Scream*.
1894 The army officer Alfred Dreyfus is convicted of espionage and deported to Devil's Island in French Guyana. Gustave Caillebotte dies.
1895 Death of Berthe Morisot. Lumière brothers invent the first cine camera and projector.
Germany: Wilhelm Röntgen discovers X-rays.
Britain: HG Wells, *The Time Machine*; Oscar Wilde, *The Importance of Being Ernest*.
1896 Acceptance by the French state of Caillebotte Bequest which includes eight works by Monet.
Britain: Death of William Morris.
1898 Zola publishes 'J'Accuse' in Georges Clemenceau's paper 'L'Aurore'. This defence of Dreyfus helps to bring about a retrial the following year. Death of Eugène Boudin.
1899 Dreyfus is released. Death of Alfred Sisley. Second Boer War (until 1902).

1900s

1900 In London February – April. Marthe Hoschedé marries Theodore Butler in October. Shows at the Exposition Centenale, part of the Exposition Universelle in Paris. In December buys a car, a Panhard-Levassor.
1901 January – April, third and final trip to work in London. Enlarges the water garden.
1903 Begins second series of Giverny garden, concentrating on the water lily pond.
1904 London pictures exhibited at Galerie Durand-Ruel in May. To Madrid with Alice and Michel in October, travelling by car to Biarritz and then by train.
1908 Visits Venice with Alice, September – December.
1909 In May the water lily series, the 'Water Landscapes', opens at Galerie Durand-Ruel.

1900 Paris Metro system opens.
Britain: Joseph Conrad, *Lord Jim*.
Austria: Sigmund Freud, *The Interpretation of Dreams*.
1901 Britain: Death of Queen Victoria. Monet watches her funeral in London. Rudyard Kipling, *Kim*. Marconi transmits first radio signals across the Atlantic.
1903 Deaths of Camille Pissarro, Gauguin and Whistler.
USA: Wright brothers make first powered flight.
1904 Entente Cordiale between Britain and France is established.
Russia: War with Japan. Anton Chekhov, *The Cherry Orchard*.
1905 Matisse shocks with Fauve works at the Salon d'Automne.
Germany: Die Brücke Expressionist group is formed in Dresden.
Switzerland: Albert Einstein formulates his special Theory of Relativity.
1906 Alfred Dreyfus is finally rehabilitated. Clemenceau first becomes Prime Minister (to 1909). Death of Paul Cézanne.
1907 Picasso paints *Demoiselles d'Avignon*.
1909 Louis Blériot flies across the English Channel.
Italy: Marinetti publishes the Futurist manifesto.

1910s

1910 Severe floods affect the water garden, after which Monet makes changes to the shape of the pond.
1911 Alice dies in May from leukaemia.
1912 Venice pictures exhibited at Galerie Bernheim-Jeune, Paris. Cataracts are diagnosed.
1913 Travels by car to Lucerne, Switzerland, with son Michel.
1914 Death of the elder son Jean, whose widow, Blanche, moves into Monet's house.
1915 Starts to build a large new studio in the garden to paint the *Grandes Décorations*.

1910 Britain: Roger Fry organises Post-Impressionist exhibition in London.
1911 Germany: Der Blaue Reiter group formed in Munich. Richard Strauss's *Rosenkavalier*.
1912 Marcel Duchamp's *Nude Descending a Staircase*. *Titanic* sinks in the North Atlantic.
1913 Marcel Proust, *Swann's Way*, the first part of *Remembrance of Things Past*. Stravinsky's *Rite of Spring*.
USA: Armory Show, New York.
1914 Outbreak of World War I.
Britain: Vorticist group is formed.
1916 Battle of Verdun. Battle of the Somme. Tanks are used for the first time.
First Zeppelin raids on Paris.
Switzerland: Dada manifestations at the Cabaret Voltaire in Zurich.
1917 Clemenceau becomes Prime Minister again (to 1920). Deaths of Degas and Rodin.
USA enters the war.
Netherlands: Mondrian and van Doesburg found *De Stijl*.
Russia: Revolution; abdication of the Tsar. Lenin becomes First Commissar of Russia and signs an armistice with Germany.
1918 Armistice is signed between Germany and the Allies.
1919 Death of Renoir.
Germany: Walter Gropius founds the Bauhaus school of art and design in Weimar.

1920s

1921 Officially agrees to present water lily paintings to France, to be housed in specially-built rooms at the Orangerie, Paris.
1923 Cataract operation, followed by a second, and then a third in July.
1924 Acquires new corrective glasses.
1925 Continues to paint the *Grandes Décorations*.
1926 Dies on 5 December, aged 86. Buried at Giverny.
1927 The *Grandes Décorations* open to the public, 17 May, at the Orangerie.

1922 Death of Paul Durand-Ruel. James Joyce's *Ulysses* is published in Paris.
Italy: Benito Mussolini takes power.
Britain: TS Eliott, *The Waste Land*.
Egypt: Discovery of Tutankhamen's tomb.
1923 Germany: Failed putsch by Adolf Hitler in Munich.
1925 First Surrealist group exhibition also in Paris.
Germany: Franz Kafka, *The Trial*.
Britain: Death of John Singer Sargent.
Russia: Serge Eisenstein's film *Battleship Potemkin*.
USA: F Scott Fitzgerald, *The Great Gatsby*.
1927 Al Jolson in *The Jazz Singer* heralds a new age of talking movies.

First published on the occasion
of the exhibition
'Monet in the 20th Century'
Royal Academy of Arts, London
23 January – 18 April 1999

The exhibition was organised
by the Museum of Fine Arts,
Boston and the Royal Academy
of Arts, London

Sponsored by

ERNST & YOUNG

Published by the Royal
Academy of Arts, London

British Library Cataloguing-
in-Publication Data
A catalogue record for this book
is available from the British Library
ISBN: 0 900946 725
(Royal Academy paperback)

Photographic reproduction
and copyright: Miranda Bennion,
Roberta Stansfield, Carola Krueger
Design: Esterson Lackersteen
Colour origination: DawkinsColour
Print: St Ives, Plymouth

The Royal Academy of Arts
is grateful to Her Majesty's
Government for its help in agreeing
to indemnify the exhibition under
the National Heritage Act 1980,
and to the Museums and Galleries
Commission for their help in
arranging this indemnity.

Photographic credits

cat 83 Bodycomb, Michael
cats 3, 28, 51, fig 1 Boston
© Museum of Fine Arts,
All Rights Reserved
cat 60 Bühler, Martin
cat 42 Carlsson, Ebbe
cat 1 Chicago, © 1998,
The Art Institute of Chicago,
All Rights Reserved
cat 18 Copenhagen, © Ole
Woldbye/Ordrupgaard
cat 38 Dallas, © Dallas Museum
of Art, All Rights Reserved
cat 25 Dayton, © 1998 The Dayton
Art Institute, All Rights Reserved
cat 85 Düren, Linke Studios
fig 3 London, Courtesy of Helly
Nahmad Gallery
cat 69, 91, fig 5 London,
© The National Gallery
cat 10 Lyon, Musée des Beaux-Arts
de Lyon/Studio Basset
cat 20 Milwaukee, Nienhuis/Walls
fig 16 Moscow, Tretyakov Gallery,
© ADAGP, Paris and
DACS, London 1998
cat 71 Nantes, AG Ville de Nantes
Musée des Beaux-Arts
fig 21 Paris, Archives Durand-Ruel
cat 86 Paris, Giraudon
cat 2 Paris, © RMN/Gerard Blot
frontispiece © Piguet, Collection
Philippe, photograph: Nadar
p 6 © Piguet, Collection Philippe
fig 2 Philadelphia, Philadelphia
Museum of Art
fig 4 Raleigh, North Carolina
Museum
cat 59 Toledo, The Toledo Museum
of Art, Ohio
cats 24, 88 Zurich, © 1998
Kunsthaus Zurich, All Rights
Reserved